SCHWETZINGEN
CASTLE
GARDENS

SCHWETZINGEN CASTLE GARDENS

Oswald Zenkner

Translated by Ernest Herbster

SIXTH EDITION
1997

K. F. SCHIMPER-VERLAG

Die Deutsche Bibliothek · CIP-Einheitsaufnahme

Schwetzingen castle gardens [a guide through the circle of the French garden and the English garden; with informations about the castle und the Rokoko theatre]
Oswald Zenker. Transl. by Ernest Herbster. - 6. ed. - Schwetzingen : Schimper, 1997
Dt. Ausg. u. d. T.: Schloßgartenführer Schwetzingen
ISBN 3-87742-113-X

© K. F. Schimper-Verlag GmbH, D-68723 Schwetzingen
1997

composed by: Schwetzinger Verlagsdruckerei GmbH, D-68723 Schwetzingen.
photographed by: Fotohaus Thomé, Kohl, Dr. Stemmle, Landesbildstelle Baden.
illustrations: Richard Bellm
aerial photograph: decontroled by Regierungspräsidium Karlsruhe
Nr. 21146-21150, 21154, 21165, 21158, 21166, 21169, 24981, 25146-25148

Index

	Buildings	Building Owner
1472	Purchase of Land	Friedrich I
1724-1731	Laying-Out	Karl Philipp
1745-1750	Birdbath	Carl Theodo
1748-1749	Northern Circle-House	
1750	Rokoko-Theater	
1753	Design for the gardens	
1753	Southern Circle-House	
1755	Neptun Fountain	
1761	Orangery	
1764	Grove of Apollo	
1766-1772	Bathhouse	
1766-1773	Temple Grove of Minerva	
1767	Stag Group	
1767	Galatea	
1773	River-Gods	
1776	Pan	
1776-1778	Temple of Botany	
1776-1779	Ruin of a Roman Waterway	
1780-1795	Mosque	
1784-1787	Temple of Mercury	
1804	Arboretum	Großherzog Karl Friedri von Baden
1823-1824	Lake	

Architect:

Bárthélemy Guibal
Allessandro Galli da Bibiena
Nicolas de Pigage
Johann Ludwig Petri
Franz Wilhelm Rabaliatti
Peter Anton von Verschaffelt
Nicolas de Pigage
Nicolas de Pigage
Nicolas de Pigage
Nicolas de Pigage
Peter Anton von Verschaffelt
Gabriel Ritter von Grupello
Peter Anton von Verschaffelt
Peter Simon Lamine
Nicolas de Pigage
Nicolas de Pigage/Friedrich Ludwig Sckell
Nicolas de Pigage
Nicolas de Pigage
Johann Michael Zeyher

Johann Michael Zeyher

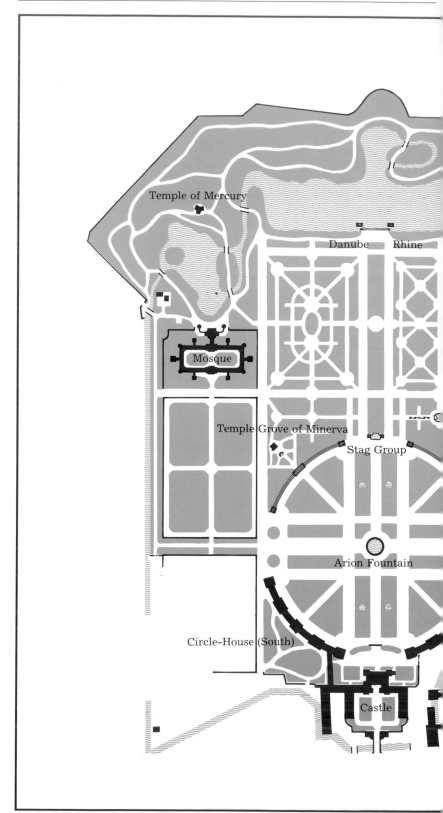

Temple of Mercury

Danube   Rhine

Mosque

Temple Grove of Minerva

Stag Group

Arion Fountain

Circle-House (South)

Castle

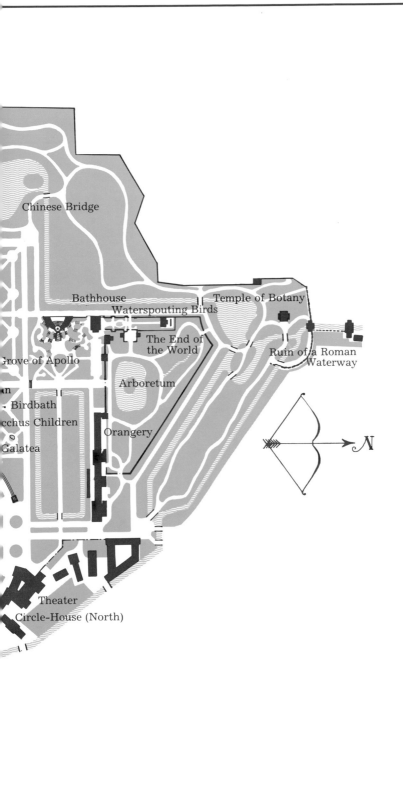

Chinese Bridge

Bathhouse

Waterspouting Birds

Temple of Botany

The End of
the World

Grove of Apollo

Ruin of a Roman
Waterway

Arboretum

Birdbath

cchus Children

Orangery

Galatea

N

Theater

Circle-House (North)

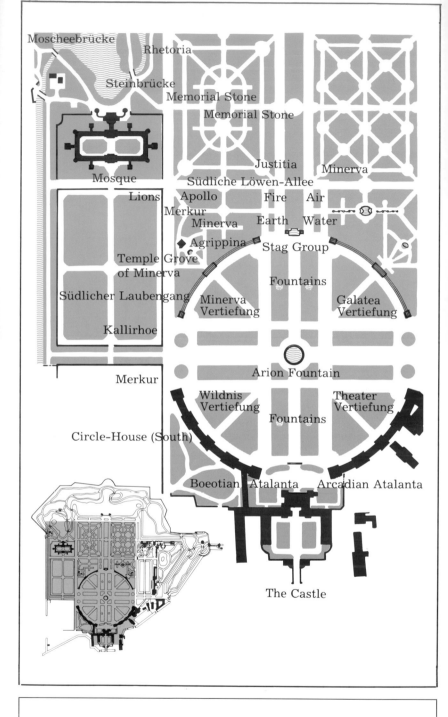

Favorite Castle

Castle

The stronghold of Schwetzingen is first mentioned in early documents in 1350. Ludwig III, Karl Ludwig, Johann Wilhelm, Karl Philipp and Carl Theodor built the castle. Today Schwetzingen castle exemplifies the age of baroque on a modest scale. (P. 20)

Arion Fountain

When one passes through the middle building, the eye alights unexpectedly on a vast formal garden area whose symmetric arrangement and fantastic proportions are incomparable. The Arion Fountain in the middle of the ground floor was created by Guibal.

Stag Group

The Group of stags is the work of von Verschaffelt. It marks the westernmost border of the gardens. This artist has portrayed a masterful and realistic representation of a deer hunt.

Temple Grove of Minerva

The temple is an original interpretation of the architecture of antiquity. The statue of Minerva, which stands inside the temple, was touched up by von Verschaffelt. The original artist was Grupello. (Page 49)

Mosque

The Mosque, created by Pigage, is the most surprising great building to be constructed and it is, from a historical point of view, a good example of the mood of the baroque age, in which the exotic was worshipped to a high degree. (Page 50)

(near Baden-Baden) is a jewel among the baroque castle buildings at the Upper Rhine-River. It was built in the 18th century for Margravine Sibylla Augusta as a summer residence. Remarkable is the interior (pottery, bone china and fayence art).

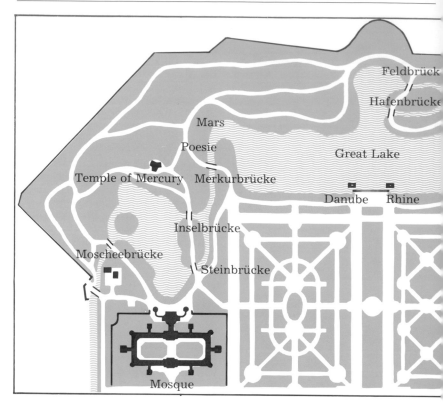

Temple of Mercury

The temple ruin, a plan of Pigage, was constructed on a cliff - like setting in a romanesque style. Various scenes out of the mythical story of Mercury were placed over the entrances to the temple. (Page 48)

River-Gods

It is at the lake that the imposing symbol figures of the Rhine and the Danube are to be found. Verschaffelt had wanted to portray the four rivers Rhine, Danube, Moselle, Maas, but he died in 1793 before he was able to complete the figures.

Rastatt Castle

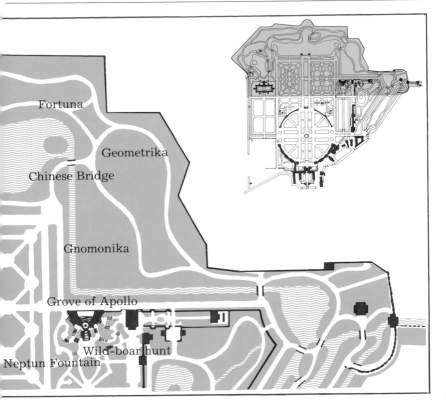

Fortuna

Geometrika

Chinese Bridge

Gnomonika

Grove of Apollo

Wild-boar hunt

Neptun Fountain

Chinese bridge

The Chinese Bridge is popularly known as the „bridge of lies". The bridge is still considered a priceless piece of the Schwetzingen gardens, a kind of chain which boldes one portion of the garden together with the other.

Grove of Apollo

The plan was conceived by Pigage. The temple is built in a strict architectural form and indicates the strong influence which classical art had on the people of the baroque age. The figure of Apollo, a work of Verschaffelt, appears to be left-handed. (Page 44)

The residence of Rastatt was built by Margrave Ludwig Wilhelm of Baden-Baden as the »new castle« according to the architecturel ideas in 1700 in Germany. Especially at this place you can find the baroque arrangement of castle and town in its original form.

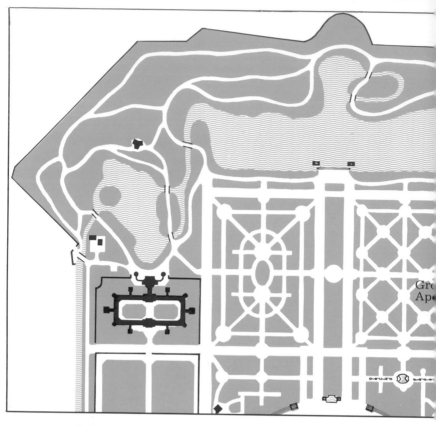

Bathhouse

Carl Theodor built a delightful little villa, a kind of summer house and a place for relaxation and quiet. Pigage was the designer. The design of this rococo architect is still considered modern to this day and shows a harmonious division of the rooms. (Page 46)

Waterspouting Birds

The waterspouting birds and the curious optical illusion known as „the end of the world" are two especially interesting spots. One has the feeling that in this particular corner of the gardens there has been a concentration of the spirit of rococo.

Bruchsal Castle

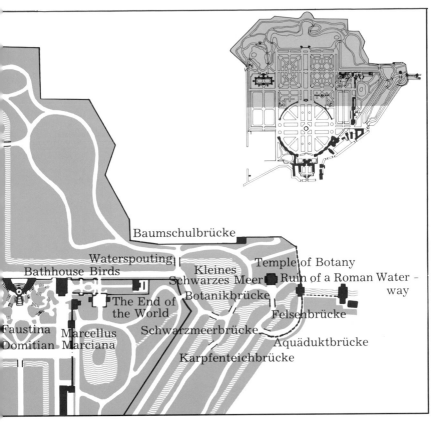

Baumschulbrücke

Waterspouting
Bathhouse Birds   Kleines   Temple of Botany
                        Schwarzes Meer   Ruin of a Roman Water -
                                                              way
                        Botanikbrücke
            The End of
            the World   Felsenbrücke

Faustina Marcellus   Schwarzmeerbrücke
Domitian Marciana   Aquäduktbrücke
                        Karpfenteichbrücke

Temple of Botany

The Temple of Botany, work of art of Pigage, a massive, cylindrical building, is supposed to resemble the mighty trunk of an oaktree. In the rear of the temple we see an allegorical figure, the goddess of Botany, the work of Carabelli, who brought it from Florence. (Page 58)

Ruin of a Roman Waterway

The Ruin is artificial and is a typical example of the spirit of the Romantic period which attempted to intensify the effects of the surrounding landscape. The clay reliefs by van den Branden were purposely antiqued. (Page 56)

The residence of Prince-Bishop Damian Hugo of Schönborn was built in the 18th century. The extraordinary centra staircase was planned by Balthasar Neumann.

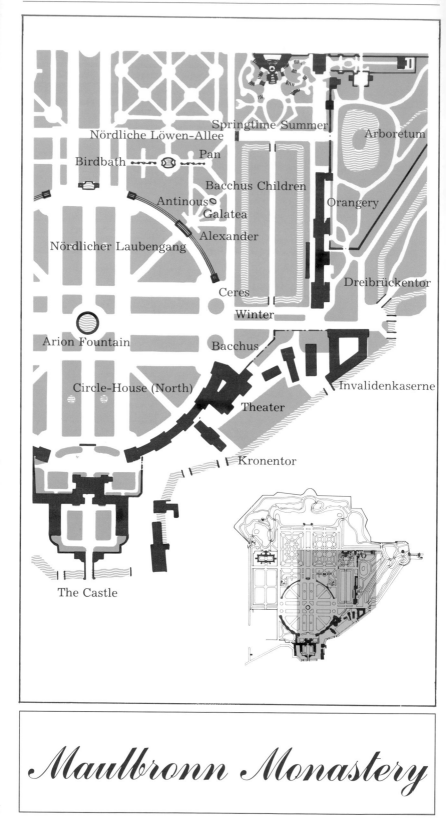

Springtime Summer

Nördliche Löwen-Allee

Arboretum

Birdbath

Pan

Bacchus Children

Antinous

Orangery

Galatea

Nördlicher Laubengang

Alexander

Dreibrückentor

Ceres

Winter

Arion Fountain

Bacchus

Circle-House (North)

Invalidenkaserne

Theater

Kronentor

The Castle

Maulbronn Monastery

Arboretum

The entrance of the Arboretum is a beautiful great handwrought iron rococo gate fashioned by the artist Rabaliatti. This prove is composed of trees gathered from all over Germany and many foreign countries. They were planted in 1804 by Zeyher.

Orangerie

We step down into a section of the gardens set somewhat lower than the other portions. To the right we see the long, low and simply built Orangery or greenhouses whose horticultural display is well worth seeing in the summer and autumn.

Pan/Birdbath

Pan created by Lamine is one of the finest works of art in the gardens (Page 67). The sculptures of lead are works of the artist Guibal. Two bubbling brooklets pass into the bond at the base of the fountain and this is known as the Birdbath.

Galatea
Bacchus Children

The wonderful piece of sculpture of Galatea is a marble statue by Grupello. At her feet we see an old Triton who is wooing her. The Bacchus children playing with a goat are a delightful rococo work of art by Linck.

Circle-Houses

The Circle-House, lying to the north, was built in 1748/49 by Bibiena. The Circle-House to the south was built in 1753 by Rabaliatti; here we find the so-called huntingroom and the ballroom, with its beautiful rococo-work.

In Maulbronn you find one the best preserved and most impressive monasteries of medieval times, north of the Alpes. It is a document of the monastic spirit of the Cisterian order which has stayed and worked at this place for 390 years until 1537.

A View of the Castle from the East

The Castle

The Castle

The broad Carl-Theodore street, which leads to the castle, is like a corridor, and the court of the castle is akin to an entrance hall to the splendid rooms of state. When one stands in the courtyard, one seems to sense systematic planning and the mathematical overtones of the baroque age, an age which is not only characterized by an overwhelming power of the imagination, but one in which such mathematical and scientific geniuses lived as Kepler, Newton and Leibniz. One is also aware of the great will-power on the part of the princes of that period to build on a monumental scale, and one is struck by the fact that the little town itself consciously retired into the background in order to elevate the residence of the Electors to its rightful position.

We step through the ostentatious gate, flanked by stately columns, to the court of honor, which is enclosed by low watchtowers. The palisades of the iron fencing stand at attention like soldiers. Within the court of honor, and immediately in front of the castle, are the renowned lilac bushes, some of which were imported from Asia. During the month of May they are in full bloom. The impact during these first few moments leads us to

the inevitable conclusion that this is a grandiose and almost theatrical setting.

The impression of the castle is one of dominance. With an inviting gesture the conspicuous side-buildings encircle the scenery. The deep-red middle building stands there like a fortress: massive, square stones, a gothic-style gate, an angular passageway, and a console decorated with figures.

The History

At the beginning of the 13th century, when the Palatinate fell the rule of the House of Wittelsbach, Schwetzingen was an imposing town composed of an upper and lower village. Even in this early period estates in the vicinity of Schwetzingen were owned by the Counts of the Palatinate. In 1288 Count of the Palatinate Ludwig II exchanged some of the estates belonging to his wife in favor of some landholdings in the vicinity of Heidelberg, including a portion of land in Schwetzingen.

The stronghold of Schwetzingen is first mentioned in early documents in 1350. It appears that by that time the Counts of the Palatinate had assured themselves of the right to use this small fort, whose original purpose apparently was to permit travelling rulers to remain there overnight while en route to the important city of Speyer. Count Ruprecht I is mentioned in these records. It was Ruprecht, who founded the University of Heidelberg in 1386. This was Germany's first university.

Ludwig III bought and exchanged several estates in Schwetzingen in 1412, 1417 und 1435. Religious peace was not established until 1485, with the settlement at Kuttenberg. Ludwig III in all probability was also the owner of the Schwetzingen stronghold, inasmuch as his testament records the fact that it was to be inherited by his two sons. Actually, this was not a stronghold in a military sense; it could not have resisted an attack for any lenght of time. Though surrounded by a moat, it would be more appropriate to call it a hunting lodge or a weekend chateau. The older son of Ludwig III was known as Frederick I the Victorious. He was populary

The Castle

open: 1.4. - 31.10. daily 10 - 19 h
terrace in the castle garden
party-rooms for 600 persons
lunch also for groups

called „Palatinate Fritz". As master of the Schwetzingen hunting lodge, he purchased most of the land with eventually became the Schwetzingen park.

About this time the Palatinate rulers were elevated by the emperor to the rank of Electors. Ludwig V (1508-1544) made some architectural changes on the hunting lodge. The two towers in the middle building of the castle as we know it today were constructed during that period. There are not many documents available which record the various changes made during that particular era.

Young Otto Henry (Elector from 1556-1559) often visited Schwetzingen, especially when the great Electoral hunts were held in the neighboring Haardt forest. Ott-Henry, as he was called, was also known as „The Big-hearted", and will always be remembered by the Heidelberg townspeople for his architectural contributions to the Heidelberg castle. There is a story that he ran off with the daughter of the mayor of Ketsch (3 miles from Schwetzingen), und that he took her to the Schwetzingen park. But the old ruins remain silent...

The Schwetzingen idyll and the quiet, modest way of life of the townspeople came to an abrupt end with the advent of the Thirty Years' War. The Protestant Elector Frederick V was forced to flee from the Palatinate. Bavarian troops plundered the town of Schwetzingen in 1621. In 1626 the cavalrymen of the famous General Tilly occupied Schwetzingen, and took away most of the food from the local inhabitants; in 1633 the Swedes sacked and burned their way through the town, and in 1635 the troops of the emperor, under the leadership of Clam Gallas, took revenge and almost completely destroyed Schwetzingen. During this period,

At the Entrance, Catholic Church in the Background

The Castle

when the wars ebbed and flowed, the castle at Schwetzingen was also destroyed, but it is impossible to say by whom. When the smoke of battle cleared away, nothing remained of the castle except the walls of stone and the arch to the roof.

Had it not been for the beautiful and gentle Fräulein Luise von Degenfeld, with whom Elector Karl Ludwig (1632-1680) fell deeply in love, the castle might never have been rebuilt. In the spring of 1657 the couple moved into their new home and lived there happily for twenty years. The „core" of the castle – remnants of a medieval water-surrounded fortress, consisting of rough-hewn stone blocks, Gothic archways, brackets with decorative figures, arcades, etc. – goes back to very early times and had remainded. The moat which once surrounded it has since been filled in.

After Karl Ludwig's death in 1680, his son, Karl II, became the ruler of the Palatinate, but died five years later without an heir. According to the law of succession, the Palatinate was to become a possession of the Palatinate-Neuburg rulers, whose court was at Duesseldorf.

Once again we find that Schwet-

zingen's fate is linked to the name of a woman. The daughter of Karl Ludwig and Charlotte, Elisabeth Charlotte, married the Duke of Orleans, brother of Louis XIV in 1671. Louis XIV intervened and claimed all of Karl Ludwig's personal properties as well as his territories in behalf of the Duke and Duchess of Orleans.

Louis' XIV armies invaded the Palatinate and Schwetzingen and its castle were burned to the ground. The Elector Johann Wilhelm (1690 – 1716) had his court architect, Breunig, a citizen of Heidelberg, rebuild the Schwetzingen castle during the years 1699 – 1715. It was not an entirely new castle, as Breunig made use of the old walls which had remained. However, the main building was enlarged considerably. In addition, a fourth story was added. After the

Arms of the House of Medici

In the French Garden

main building was completed, construction was begun on the wings und connecting structures. These, together with two guardhouses at the entrance, complete the imposing area known as the Court of Honor.

Today's Schwetzingen castle exemplifies the age of baroque on a modest scale. And since it was necessary to make use of the older walls which had remained und which date back to earlier periods in order to reduce the cost, the castle is not pure baroque. Yet, the form of the structure is such that, with the additional effect of color, the castle becomes a typical example of baroque architecture, whose chief characteristics are the use of imagination, movement of forms, and color. At the entrance to the Court of Honor, which is closed off by a beautiful, handwrought baroque gate, there are two pillars on which are the coats of arms of the Palatinate and the House of Medici (the second wife of Johann Wilhelm was an Italian lady by the name of Anna Maria of Tuscany).

The Elector Karl Philipp (1716 – 1742), Johann Wilhelm's successor, temporarily resided in the Schwetzingen castle. During this brief period of residence there, he added several touches to the park. For one thing, he transferred the Orangery from Duesseldorf, and it is reported that the park bore a strong resemblance to an orange and lemon plantation. He also built an attractive greenhouse in the middle of the gardens, where the main fountains are now located. The walls of this buildung were decorated whith precious porcelain from Delft. A covered corridor connected the greenhouse with the castle. But all this has since disappeared.

The Elector died without any heirs, and so the rule of the House of Palatinate-Neuburg came to an end. In 1743 the Elector Carl Theodore took over the reins of government, and thus began Schwetzingen's Golden Age.

In May, 1753, Carl Theodore approved of the plans of courtgardener, Johann Ludwig Petri, to build the park. Before the end of that year, thousands of trees began arriving from Utrecht, among them 3411 linden trees, within a period of more than two hundred years, have developed into lovely promenades.

Carl Theodor died 1799. His state did not survive him for long. The fire of the French Revolution was destroying the way of life of the ancient regime. When Max I Joseph of Palatinate-Zweibrücken-Birkenfeld, born in Schwetzingen on 27 May 1756, ascended the throne after Carl Theodore's death, the fate of the Palatinate was already sealed. The Treaty of Basel (1795, between Prussia and France), the Treaty of Campoformio (1797, between Austria and France), and the Paris Treaty ratified by Baden in 1797, all contained secret provisions regarding the turning over to

An unusual View of the Main Building of the Castle

France of the left bank of the Rhine. The princes affected by this move were to be compensated by territorial reparations on the right bank. The Peace of Lunéville, 9. February 1801, was no more than the formal death knell for the Palatinate. At a meeting of deputies on 25. February 1803, the treaty clauses were called into effect and the Palatinate with is princely residences at Heidelberg, Mannheim and Schwetzingen, fell to the State of Baden. 1835 the Castle was renovated. Lilacs were planed. 1924 the garden was opened for the public. During the years 1927 – 1929 the castle was completely renovated. When the Americans arrived in 1945, the castle was requisitioned temporarily for use as troop billets.

During the last few years, extensive restoration and repair work has been necessary on almost all the buildings in the Schwetzingen park; a good deal of this work, including the painstaking restoration of the stucco-work decorations, was carried out by the sculptor August Dursy, who resides in Schwetzingen.

The wing in the south (with the kitchen) was pulled down in the middle of the sixties and rebuilt for the „Fachhochschule für Rechtspflege" with a boarding-school. The fiscal-office is using the northern wing.

Historical plans of the garden were realized 1973/74. Now the garden again possesses the charme of the Rokoko, colored coverings are harmonizing with pretty pictorial works and blossoms. The English Garden was rebuilt and newly planted. The fourteen bridges were renovated, the canals, the shores of the lake, new pathes and plants were included into this picture of this very attractive part of the English Garden.

The Castle

The Interior

The bedroom of Elector Carl Theodor.

From 1975 until 1991 there was a careful and historical restauration of the castle rooms. A tour through the different rooms shows the likeness of the way of living. You find costly furnished cabinets as well as cloakrooms, closets for the ladies-in-waiting and the lackeys. The remarkable feature of Schwetzingen is the original furnishing of the rooms.

The rooms can be visited daily on guided tours except on Mondays.

Groundplan of the Castle – Ground Floor

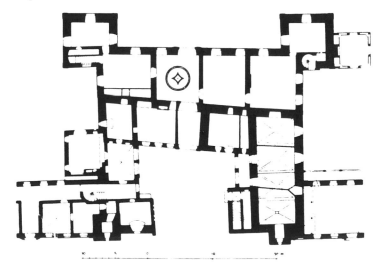

The Circle-Houses

The Circle-House lying to the North

The circle-house, lying to the north, was built in 1748/49 according to the plans of Alessandro Galli da Bibiena; the circle-house to the south was built in 1753 by Franz Wilhelm Rabaliatti, who had already worked with Bibiena a few years prior to that in connection with the construction of the Jesuit church in Mannheim. When Nicolas de Pigage came to Schwetzingen in 1749 (the year of the German Poet, Goethe's, birth), plans were made for the rebuilding of the castle. These, however, never materialized. The Orangery was placed into the northern circle-house at that time, while richly decorated festival rooms were built into the southern circle-house. Here we find the so-called hunting-room and the ballroom, with its beautiful rococo stucco-work.

The Circle-House lying to the South

The Theater

The Schwetzingen theater is one of the most important sights in the park. It is located behind the northern circle-house. Carl Theodore had ordered his court architect as early as 1746 to build a little theater so that French comedy could be brought to Schwetzingen. For some unknown reason the order was not carried out at that time.

Four years later, when Nicolas de Pigage became the chief architect, the theater was built within a few month' time. The original estimate of the cost of the building was 5,900 gulden, but it turned out to be about four times as expensive.

The castle theater opened in the fall of 1752 with a performance of the musical intermezzo „Porsorg-nacco". In 1753 Ignaz Holzbauer, from Stuttgart, was called to Schwetzingen as court composer and music director, and many of his own operas (in the Italian „buffo" manner) were premiered at the castle theater. It was also in 1753 that Voltaire visited Schwetzingen for the first time; he remained there for two weeks as the guest of his long-time friend, the Elector, and his comedies were performed in the castle theater before an enthusiastic audience. During the summer of 1758, the French poet returned to Schwetzingen for a second visit. On 30 September 1762, the castle theater presented the first performance of his tragedy „Olympie", directed by his former secretary, Collini, who had found a position at the Schwetzingen court. On 29 May 1768, shortly before his death, Voltaire wrote to Collini: „Before I die I want to fulfill one

Festival-Ballet »Tanzstunden«

obligation and enjoy one consolation – I want to see Schwetzingen again. This idea has taken possession of my soul." We know from contemporary literature that the castle theater in Schwetzingen was the scene of elaborate and splendid productions, particularly of large-scale ballets.

As Germany's own poets and dramatists gained in importance and renown and their works began to replace the plays of the French comedy writers, the Elector Carl Theodore was one of the first champions of the native drama for Schwetzingen. In the autumn of 1770, much to the annoyance of his wife, Elisabeth Auguste, he dismissed his French theater company... The Mozarts operas were not performed in Schwetzingen during Carl Theodore's lifetime. On 18 July 1763, however, Mozart – as a seven-year old prodigy – gave a concert in the circle-house together with his father and his sister, Nannerl. His father, Leopold Mozart, writes the following regarding the concert: „The orchestra is without doubt the best in Germany. All young people and all of them well-bred – neither drunkards, gamblers, nor advocates of loose living, so that their conduct as well as their performance is

Cartouche above the Stage

worthy of the highest praise. My children set all Schwetzingen in motion..." In 1774 Christoph Willibald von Gluck visited Schwetzingen as the guest of the Elector. In his memoirs, the painter Mannlich reports that on one occasion the composer, sitting behind the royal couple in the second row of the theater after a somewhat heavy lunch, fell asleep during a performance of Johann Christian Bach's pastoral opera „Amor Vincitore".

After Carl Theodore moved his residence to Munich, the Schwetzingen theater was used only rare-

The Entrance of the Theatre

ly, when he happened to be there for a visit. Even during the period of the Grand Duchy Baden, the theater was seldom in operation. The last gala performance during the latter period took place in September 1840, in honor of the military maneuvers of the Eight Army Corps. Its headquarters were in Schwetzingen, which meant that a number of German princes were in residence there and as a result, the castle theater was used for several performances.

After this nothing more was done to keep the theater in good repair, and it gradually fell into ruin. Since its renovation and reopening in 1937, the Schwetzingen rococo theater has become the scene of the world-famous annual music festivals. After World War II it was also used occasionally for guest performances by companies from nearby cities. In 1952, after the interruption occasioned by the war years, the Schwetzingen Festivals were resumed with the performance of several Gluck operas, produced with new stage sets designed especially for the festival. The 1952 festival was arranged at the suggestion and with the financial assistance of the South German Broadcasting Company, Stuttgart, to commemorate the 200th anniversary of the castle theater.

The technical equipment of the theater, and particularly its lighting equipment, was extremely modern and included all the newest „gadgets". In the spring of 1952, the theater heating plant was renovated so that the theater, originally intended for summer use only, can now be utilized during the winter as well.

A second staircase was built in 1959 on the eastern side. In the seventies the state of Baden-Württemberg renovated the stage. 1974 the theater was opened to the public again.

Foyer of the Theater

The Interior

The Auditorium

Ceiling Fresco

Pigage found a happy solution for the utilizations of space in the summer theater; the galleries with their private boxes, the lobby, and the rehearsal rooms are all arranged to make the most of the available space. The stage itself is rather unusual – the main stage is nearly sixteen meters wide and twenty meters deep, and in 1762 a rear stage was added with exits leading into the gardens, so that the over-all depth of the stage was increased to over thirty-four meters. As a result, the illusion of perspective achieved by the stage scenery could be extended into the natural perspective of the park landscape beyond. The stage and auditorium are built on a slight incline, rising in opposite directions from the center of the theater. Underneath the stage and in the flies is housed the complicated stage machinery, consisting of huge

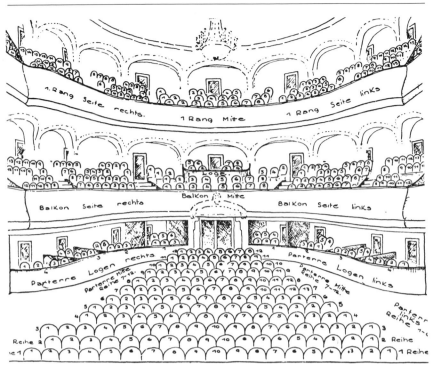

The Seating Arrangement

drums, winches, pulleys, and mechanically operated tradpoors, which permit not only rapid changes of scenery but also some extremely theatrical stage effects. During the course of the following centuries, the castle theater gradually fell into disrepair and was no longer used. In 1936 the work of restoration was begun, with careful attention to the finely spirit of rococo architecture, and the theater – completely renovated – was reopened on 10 October 1937.

The auditorium presents a fascinating and wholly charming picture. The balustrades along the balconies, curving slightly upwards towards the rear of the house, are constructed in the form of a lyre. The columns are richly decorated with stuccowork and carving and support graceful arches which give the room an illusion of depth and of rhythmic unity. This rhythmic grace of style is characteristic of the auditorium as a whole and conveys an impression of life and motion. The colors adorning the balustrades, columns, and arches – beige, white grey, and gold – are indicative of the decorative richness and graceful proportion of baroque architecture. Rococo touches, which abound in the Schwetzingen theater, lack the over-rich, elaborate, and luxuriant detail which is so typical of baroque ornamentation. As a matter of fact, Pigage went even further than rococo and decorated the theater with motifs (draperies, acanthus, leaves, and lion-heads) closely associated with Classicism and harking back to the Italian Renaissance. The elaborately proportioned proscenium, with its blue and grey marbled pillars with gilded capitals, the richly carved emblems decorating the gilded grill-

The Stage

work of the two on-stange boxes, and the proscenium arch with its electoral coat of arms, add to the

Moulding Sculptures

pomp and splendor of the auditorium.

The stage curtain, with its beautyfully stylized representation of the temple of the sun from Mozart's Flute (taken from an original water-color by the scene-painter J. Quaglio, of Mannheim and Schwetzingen fame, and designed by O. Mueller, Godesberg), gives an illusion of space and serves to bring the magic of the stage into the auditorium. The new ceiling decoration, painted by Carolus Vocke in 1957 and representing Apollo and the nine Muses – an allegory of Schwetzingen as the Palatinate Temple of the Muses – provides a fitting crown for the whole. The pastel colors and the delicacy of the figures call to mind the lines of Schiller's „Eleusinian Festival" (Das Eleusische Fest).

The painting, a free composition in which the observer can detect the charming figures of the boy, Mozart, and his sister, Nannerl, on the Schwetzingen Mount Olympus, fits perfectly into the style of the auditorium. Its delicate color harmony and the airy lightness of its figures bespeak an intuitive feeling on the part of the artist for the graceful charm of the Schwetzingen castle theater.

Even more amazing are the new stage decorations, created in 1957 from designs prepared by the Karlsruhe stage-designer, Trude Karrer, and carried out with the help of the scenepainter Kappler, from the theater at Baden-Baden. The front part of the stage has been transformed into a baroque salon whose ceiling and wall pillars are richly decorated with stuccowork. The rear wall is formed by a curtain on which is painted the reproduction of a tapestry (The Transformation of Jupiter) from the collection of Cardinal Damian Hugo von Schoenborn of Bruchsal. When this curtain is raised, the eye is led along a seemingly endless landscape of arcades and shrubs, interspersed with dainty statues, to a Glorietta with a fountain in front of it. The almost uncanny illusion of depth achieved is the result of painstaking work with spirit-level and drawingboard to create the ex-act perspective needed to make the view seem to be endless. It is without doubt one of the most impressive sights in Europe.

The Festival

The Festival takes place in april and may. The „Schwetzinger Festspiele GmbH" is the organizer of operas, concerts and stageplays with famous ensembles and well-known artists. (Premiere of operas by Britten, Egk, Fortner and revisions of operas by Rossini, Purcell, Gluck, Paisiello.) Recordings of many of these performances have been broadcasted not only by the German Broadcasting Companies, but also by many foreign stations including USA, Japan, Australia and Russia. Since several years also the Television stations are interested in the Schwetzingen Festival: in 1987 the first fulltime recording of an opera („Die Italienerin in Algier") was on TV in whole western Europe via Eurovision.

„Der Barbier von Sevilla"

The Castle and the Circle framing the French Garden

The Castle Gardens

The French Garden

When one passes through the middle building, the eye alights unexpectedly on a vast formal garden area whose symmetric arrangement, fantastic proportions, as well as architectural and geometrical links, are incomparable. The wonderful view down the broad middleaxis, is momentarily interrupted by a small body of water bordered by a group of stately stags which are sculptured in stone. This pond is imbedded in the center of the green lawns, and from a distance it gives the appearance of a glistening jewel. The view then narrows into a thin line toward the west, and seems to disappear into the eternity of heaven. The underlying princi-

ple of the baroque garden is shown to perfection here. It is the use of grand dimensions and complex, artistic forms, which have all been predetermined on a great drawing-board.

The visitor, who strolls into the garden, almost has the feeling that some unseen hand is gently pushing him forward, or perhaps that the garden itself is leading him on. One hardly notices the low steps into the gardens which have been sunk down very slightly by means of three terraces. One walks leisurely along the middle path, or perhaps along the shady promenade, admiring the artistic fountains whose rhythmic streams of water cross one another in a playful manner. And now we find

The French Garden with the Arion Fountain

ourselves in front of the Arion fountain created by the sculptor from Lorraine, Barthélemy Guibal. The four smaller fountains situated out in the lawns were also the work of this excellent artist.

Carl Theodore acquired these art treasures from the estate of King Stanislaus I, who reigned in Nancy and Lunéville during the period 1735 – 1766. It is said that he paid according to their weight at the rate of 10 sous to the pound.

We are standing in the center of an immense circle which encloses the entire garden area. From the point of view of architecture and landscaping, the gardens achieve a complete sense of harmony by means of the semi-circular buildings to the right and the left of the castle which join in a second half-circle created by the shady promenades. No other baroque garden in the world has this great, unique circle, within which we experience this charming interplay between the open and closed landscape, between light and shade, between one symmetrical form and another.

But, not only is the fountain in the geometrical center of the garden, it is also the symbolical center – the center of an autocratic power and a dynamic way of life dedicated to the furtherance of pomp

Urn in the French Garden

and splendor, to beauty and the arts. The radiations from this center went out in all directions to the ends of the earth.

A new and rather confusing optical illusion holds the visitor fast at

Pergola in the French Garden

the little pond next to the stags. At this point the garden seems to be forged to the sky by means of an invisible band. This illusion is created by the fact that the middle-axis runs exactly between two points, the Königstuhl in the east, on which is situated the Heidelberg Castle; and in the west, the Kalmit, which is the highest mountain in the Haardt. This latter chain of low mountains formed the western border of the Palatinate power. Doesn't it seem as though this garden, in itself an artistic portrayal of a great world-theater, lay in the center of the world? One also has the impression of a huge arm extending far over the Rhine.

Before we wander on, let us take one more look around. Symmetry and harmony compose the secret of these marvelous gardens. The castle, the circular houses, the covered walks, the pictorial works, and the plastic figures all blend together into one harmonious whole.

Not only do the beaux arts play their part in this cheerful setting, but nature also is important and brings the whole into perfect accord. The carefully placed trees sparkle in the sunlight, spaying fountains glimmer in the soft tones of the rainbow colors, colorful blossoms dot the peripheries of the lawns, the scent of roses is in the air in the neighborhood of the arcades, shadows sweep over the glowing flowerbeds and the bright facade of the castle throws a reflection across the gardens.

Lower Transverse

The English Garden

Bridge in the English Garden

A canal divides the English Garden from the main portion of the gardens done in the French style. The English Garden is situated on the western edge of the park. One notices the difference immediately. Here, in place of the formal and artificial, we have a completely natural setting. The landscape in this area is a mixture of trees, bushes, and meadows, all growing more or less to suit themselves. One hardly has the feeling of being in a garden at all. The paths no longer run in a straight line, but rather in gentle curves. The atmosphere of the romantic period surrounds us here. With every few steps we are offered a different view. Here and there we see the artistic play between ligth and shade. At this point there does not seem to be any barrier to the garden; it appears to go on and on into the adjacent countryside.

The Area around the Lake

„Feeding Place" at the Lake

The area around the lake, built on a rather grand scale, permitted the gardens to be rounded of in a splendid manner. From the Chinese bridge our view sweeps across of the huge chestnut trees, to the glistening waters of the great pond which, incidentally, is a popular place for skating in the winter. The French portion of the gardens is closed off by the promenade of linden trees.

Originally, in place of the lake, there was a rectangular basin of water which was surrounded by a wall. In 1823, Zeyher, then director of the gardens, suggested that the wall be removed in order to make room for a larger lake with natural banks. This was an ideal solution and improved the landscape materially. The middle section of the east bank of the lake was changed somewhat in 1928 with the addition of a low wall and a set of steps which lead down into the water.

The Arboretum

The Entrance of the Arboretum

The entrance of the Arboretum is a beautiful handwrought iron rococo gate fashioned by the artist, Rabaliatti. This grove is composed of trees gathered from all over Germany and many foreign countries. They were planted in 1804 at the direction of the grand duke Karl Friedrich of Baden. The director of the garden at that time was the wellknown architect Johann Michael Zeyher.

Peacocks

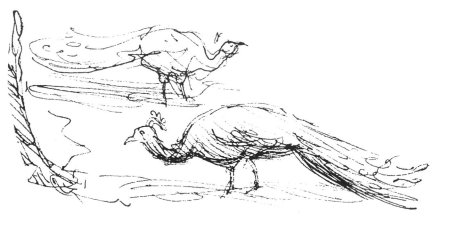

The Grove of Apollo

The Grove of Apollo

One of the most impressive and beautiful sections of the Schwetzingen gardens is the area around the Temple of Apollo. It is a kind of

The Sculpture of Apollo

oasis in a labyrinth of surprises. This plan was conceived by Pigage. The first works of sculpture were ordered in 1762. In 1764 construction of the garden area was begun, and in 1776 it was not quite completed. We find here that several landscape styles are masterfully interwoven. The basic spirit is that of the rococo period. And yet we also sense the influence of the English garden style, a more open and more natural landscape. We have a sunken garden which is surrounded by sphinxes. At one end is a small, artificial hill, representing Mt. Parnassus, which was sacred to Apollo and the Muses. Behind the hill of Parnassus the Temple rises. It is built in a strict architectural form, and indicates the strong influence which classical art had on the people of the baroque age. Twelve Ionic columns hold up a simple cupola. The slim and youthful figure of Apollo, a work of Verschaffelt, is seen standing on a pedestal in the middle of the temple. The athletic figure of the young god is impressive. However, Wilhelm Heinse (1746 – 1803) once wrote that the left-handed god had a miserable-looking set of buttocks.

It is true that the Schwetzingen Apollo appears to be left-handed. Friedrich Schiller, the great German poet, who also visited Schwetzingen while in Mannheim, once wrote the floowing rather sarcastic lines: „He governs the lyre with the left hand; is it any wonder that he plays in a left-handed manner in this vicinity?" These words were not so much directed at Schwetzingen, as they were against the celebrated actor and poet, Iffland, possibly also at a whole group of rather mediocre personalities who were writing for the Mannheim theater at the time.

According to one anecdote, Verschaffelt replied wittily to his critics that Apollo would have been a miserable little God, if he had been unable to play the lyre with both hands. The view is enhanced by means of a miniature cascade, over the top of which two water nymphs have been placed, who are holding a pitcher from which water is being poured. At the rear of the temple there are broad steps and a large terrace which is closed off by means of an attractive lattice-work ornamented with reproductions of the sun.

Detail of the Grove of Apollo: Nymphs

This entire scence originally served as a natural theater. The terrace in front of the fountain served as the stage, and the somewhat deeper-lying great terrain surrounded by the six sphinxes was used by the spektators, and both sides were screened of by means of lattice-work.

The Grove of Apollo was renovated in 27 months (1,9 Mio DM). Close to the Temple of Apollo, on the hill, is a small stone grotto in which we find a lead sculpture of a wild boar being chased by dogs. This is another work by Guibal. Along the paths in this vicinity are six busts of stone by Konrad Linck. It is believed that they portray the following personalities: the head of a gladiator; the Greek philosopher, Solon; the emperor, Domitian; Trajan's sister, Marcina Augusta, Marcellus, the adopted son of emperor Augustus; and Faustina, the wife of emperor Antonius.

Detail of the Grove of Apollo: Lattice-Work ornamented with Reproductions of the Sun

The Bathhouse

The Bathhouse

Just next door to the grove of Apollo, Carl Theodore built a delightful little villa, a kind of sum-

The Bathroom

mer house and a place for relaxation and quiet. It is the so-called Bathhouse. Again it was Pigage who was the designer.

The open area in front of the Bathhouse is adorned with a small fountain depicting a bowl over which the water plays so that it has the appearance of a water bell. This bowl is known as the „bowl of lentils". Next to it is the so-called porcelain house whose walls have been decorated with tiles from Delft.

Without doubt the Bathhouse is the most significant building in the Schwetzingen gardens, from an architectural point of view. The design of this rococo architect is still considered modern to this day, and shows a masterful and harmonious division of the rooms. Two halfcircular entrance halls, on the right and on the left, lead to the middle room which is topped by a dome-like ceiling. In the southern entrance hall (which runs in the direction of the Temple of Apollo) there are two plastercast works of art by Peter Anton Verschaffelt

and Ildefonso. The one by Verschaffelt is a reproduction of
Cupid, the other by Ildefonso is
that of a faun. In the northern entrance hall we find Idolino and
Apollino Tribuna. The elliptical
middle room of the Bathhouse is
furnished in a splendid manner.
There are four figures of women,
representing the four seasons, each
one standing in a niche and
overlooking a console table. These
are again by Verschaffelt. These
sculptures are covered with gold
leaf and are among the best works
of this versatile artist. The upper
portion of the wall is divided by
means of relief work between
which square windows have been
set. The floor is made of bluish-
withe marble whose designs reflect
the elliptical lines of the room.
Then there is a ceiling painting by
Guibal which portrays Aurora and
the fleeing night. On each side of
the middle room there are square
antechambres which, in turn, are
adjoined to rectangular chambers.
On the east side there is a Chinese

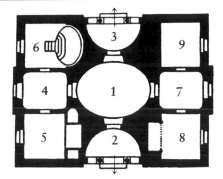

The Plan of the Bathhouse

1 Great Drawing-Room   6 Bathingroom
2 Southern Entrance   7 Antechamber
3 Northern Entrance   8 Writing Room
4 Antechamber   9 Chinese Room
5 Room of Rest and Quiet

Interior of the Drawing-Room

room with Chinese tapestry. Opposite this room is the so-called writ-
ing-room in which there is a series
of landscape paintings by Fer-
dinand Kobell. These Schwetzingen idylls are among the best work
of Kobell, and are well worth a visit. The rooms of the Bathhouse are
further enhanced by some very ex-
quisite rosewood panelings. On the
western side of the Bathhouse we
come to the room designated for
rest and quiet. It is also decorated
with beautiful Chinese silk tapestry. The bathingroom itself is
equipped in a really princely style.

   The deep marble basin again is in
the design of an ellipse. The water-
pipes are artistically decorated
with four snaks and an urn, the
work of Linck. The stucco artist of
the court, Josef Pozzi created some
magnificent work. He also used
semi-precious stones and mirrors
to add to the sumptuousness of this
room. We could go on and on in our
description of this special jewel in
the Schwetzingen gardens, but
there is not space enough in this
guidebook. In any event, so far as
the Bathhouse is concerned, we
might well say: description is nothing – to experience it is everything.

The Temple of Mercury

The Temple of Mercury

Sckell, the co-worker of Pigage decided to dig up the ground in front of the Mosque so as to create a small pond. The earth which he had dug up he then had transported to a site opposite, where he built a small hill on top of which the ruin of the Temple of Mercury was built. The original plan had been to build a monument to the Egyptian king, Sesostris. However, this never materialized. The temple ruin, again the plan of Pigage, was constructed on a cliff-like setting, in a romanesque style. Various scenes out of the mythical story of Mercury were placed over the entrances to the temple.

The Temple Grove of Minerva

The builder of the garden here showed his reverence for antiquity, and thereby elevated his own stature. Minerva, as the ancient Roman goddess of wisdom, technical skill, and invention, has been given a special place in the gardens. She is portrayed in a frieze directly under the roof of the temple, leaning on a shield with a Gorgon's head on it; the plan of the park is spread out in front of her, and we can be certain that the goddess has given her approval. The temple itself is not an imitation of some classical building. It is an original interpretation of the architecture of antiquity. Eight columns support the portion of the roof which juts out. An additional eight columns hold up the inside room. The coffered ceiling is decorated with rosettes. The statue of Minerva, which stands inside the temple, was touched up by Verschaffelt. The original artist was Grupello. The altar sculptures are also the work of Verschaffelt. In 1951 the temple was in such poor condition that it had to be restored.

The Temple Grove of Minerva

The Mosque with the Corridors for Prayers

The Mosque

The Entrance to the Area around the Mosque

The final portions of the baroque and rococo park were constructed in 1780. These were the so-called Turkish Garden and the area around the Temple of Mercury located in the English Garden.

The area around the Mosque was remodeled in 1974. The Mosque built by Pigage is probably the most interesting and surprising bit of architecture in the entire gardens. According to reports, it cost a total of 120 000 gulden, a tidy sum of money for those times. This particular building is the best example of the versatility and ability of the architect, Pigage, who, in step with the times, moulded the various styles and works of art together into an excellent reproduction of the world, in miniature.

And so from one generation to the next, as the artistic tastes gradually changed, the Mosque and its architecture was either denounced or praised by the art critics. However, these quarrels among the crit-

Epigrams at the Wall

ics were primarily of interest to the art historians, and not to the vast public which visited the gardens. As a matter of fact, it had also been said, and nowadays one still reads occasional articles to the same effect, that the Schwetzingen Mosque is a copy of the mosque in Mecca or even of the Taj Mahal in Agra, India. A comparison of the photographs of these buildings would quickly show that this is not so. Furthermore, it is not an imitation of any other islamic building. The oriental scholar from Schwetzingen, Professor Alfons Schachner, stated that it was an imaginative transfer of the oriental idea into the grand middle-European language of art of the 18th century. Although the basic character of the architecture is baroque, one also sees the influence of the early Romantic period which was just developing after the middle of the 18th century. The Mosque is the final, important building to be constructed, and it appears that it was Carl Theodore's plan to make this the crowning achievement in a park which had already become famous throughout Europe. He wanted it to be a monumental work, unique, splendid, and extraordinary.

We, who live in the 20th century, react to this piece of architecture just as the builders wanted us to: the Mosque creates the illusion of a strange, foreign atmosphere, something definitely oriental, the setting for a fairytale out of „The Arabian Nights".

The Mosque really is a fairytale building, and from a historical point of view, a good example of the mood of the baroque age, in which the exotic was worshipped to a high degree.

The red facade of the Mosque unexpectedly comes into view from behind the protecting shield of trees. This quick moment of surprise was cleverly calculated into the plans of the builders. The cupola and its minarets stretch gracefully towards the sky. And when we step through one of the side-gates into the courtyard, we are completely fascinated by the magic of the orient. The entire courtyard is surrounded by a corridor for prayer. The latticework of wood, giving the corridor the necessary privacy, is the work of expert craftsmen. To make the whole structure even more realistic, there are rooms for the priests and for washing. The inside of the Mosque is just as genuine. The floor has been laid with marble slabs, and eight pilasters (columns) hold up the cornice of the cupola. The walls are embellished with stucco artwork, goldleaf, and paintings. Not only the Zouaves and the Turks, who were prisoners of war in the Schwetzingen army hospital in 1870 – 1871, admired the Mosque, but also the Shah of Persia, who was a guest of the Grand

The Interior of the Mosque

The Mosque

Duke of Baden in 1889. In 1945, when the American troops entered the area, they were so impressed by the building, that it was soon converted into a club for soldiers. In earlier times, the courtyard was used for open air theater performances. Mozart's „Abduction from the Seraglio" probably never had a more beautiful setting. During recent years the Mosque has occasionally been used by Mohammedan groups for religious services. Quotations from the Koran are inscribed on the ceiling of the Mosque, as well as on the innermost round wall, and on the outer walls.

The Observatory

On the place of the orangerie the Elector Carl Theodore had a small observatory built in 1762. The instruments were imported from England. The following year it was moved to the roof of the castle.

The Jesuit scholar, Christian Mayer, was the director of the observatory for several years. Ten years later it was moved to Mannheim.

The Orangerie

Orangery Steps

Coming from Pan, we continue walking along to the right, crossing the chestnut tree promenade, passing two lions, and then step down into a section of the gardens set somewhat lower than the other portions. To the right we see the long, low, and simply built Orangery, or greenhouses, whose horticultural display is well worth seeing in the summer and autumn.

The Ruin of a Roman Waterway

The Ruin of a Roman Waterway

At the northern border of the English Garden area, we see the old ruin of a Roman waterway. It does not take a great deal of imagination to picture in one's mind an old Roman landscape dominated by a waterfort and an aquaduct. The Clay reliefs by van den Branden, set in the old stonework, were purposely antiqued. The ruin itself is artificial, and is a typical example of the spirit of the Romantic period which attempted to intensify the effects of the surrounding land-scape. Nowadays the ruin is covered over with ivy so that one really has the impression that it is an old Roman ruin dating back 2000 years ago.

From the top of the waterfort one has an excellent view of the Rhine plain and also the Bergstraße beyond Heidelberg. Just outside the gardens is an old millrace which supplied the pressure for the various fountains in that portion of the garden (now done by machinery). During the time of Carl Theodore

The Clay Reliefs

the old mill was also used to grind up bones which were used to fertilize the flowerbeds.

The main waterworks which supply the water and the pressure for the various fountains in other parts of the park is situated in the vicinity of the castle. It is an ingenious set-up of large waterwheels which drive a series of pumps, and stems from the 18th century.

In 1952 a large, new tank was built into the top of the watertower. The natural water-pressure made it possible for the Arion fountain to send jets of water as high as fifty feet into the air.

The Roman Waterway

The Temple of Botany

The Temple of Botany

In the northwestern portion of the English Garden, in the Arboricum Theodoricum, we come to the Temple of Botany, another work of art of Pigage. The massive, cylindrical building is supposed to resemble the mighty trunk of an oaktree. The temple is flanked by two sphinces. There are no windows, so that the only light comes in from the open doorway and a cupola of glass. Looking through the entrancedoor to the rear of the temple, we see an allegorical figure set in small niche in the wall, the goddess of Botany, the work of

The Temple of Botany

Francesco Carabelli, who brought it from Florence: to the right and left are two marble vases, probably by the same artist. Hanging over four altars in wall-relief form, are medaillon portraits of the natural scientists, Plinius, Theophratus, Tournefort, and Linné. Above these are some more works of art in stucco by Pozzi. These depict the four seasons and the zodiac. The ornate urns on each side of the temple are by Mathäus van den Branden.

The Entrance of the Temple of Botany

The Fountains

The Arion Fountain

The Arion Fountain in the middle of the ground floor was created by Barthelemy Guibal.

Out on the lawns, which enclose the Arion fountain, there are four urns of white marble set on pedestals. They were created by the Italian sculptor, Carabelli: their flat reliefs represent the arts and sciences.

The Arion Fountain

The Birdbath

We leave the group of stags, and pass along to the section of the gardens on the righthand side. The path broadens in a circular effect, and in the middle we come to an attractive fountain. The sculptures of lead are works of the artist Barthélemy Guibal, and they came from the park which belonged to the titular sovereign, Stanislaus, in Lunéville. Two bubbling brooklets pass into the pond at the base of the fountain, and this is known as the birdbath. This, in turn, is surrounded by eight attractive lead vases.

The Birdbath

The Neptun Fountain

Along the stone walls which surrounded the grove of Apollo we find the Neptune fountain, by Verschaffelt.

The Neptun Fountain

The Stag Group

The Stag Group

The group of stags is the work of Peter Anton von Verschaffelt. It marks the westernmost border of the gardens. This artist has portrayed a masterful and realistic representation of a deer hunt.

The Waterspouting Birds and The End of the World

On leaving the Bathhouse, perhaps we, too, have that sense of the labyrinthian which Daidalos, the forefather of all the creative arts, was able to conjure up in his own fabulous garden on the island of Crete. Now suddenly we come upon two especially interesting spots, having walked beneath an arbor covered with wild grapevines. These are the waterspouting birds (renewed in 1929) and the curios optical illusion known as „the end of the world". One has the feeling once again that in this particular corner of the gardens there has been a concentration of the spirit of rococo with all of its exquisiteness and effects of surprise.

Details of the Waterspouting Birds

The Chinese Bridge

The Chinese Bridge

The Chinese Bridge is populary known as the „bridge of lies"; but, although many a lover may have given his promise and then broken it, the little bridge has not tumbled down to this day. However, to be on the safe side, the bridge was rein-forced in 1951. The bridge is still considered a priceless piece of the Schwetzingen gardens, a kind of chain which holds one portion of the garden together with the other, a place intimate chats and for lovers to stand and dream together!

The Chinese Bridge

The Sculptures

Agrippina

Between the statues of Minerva and Mercury near the temple grove of Minerva we find a sizable portrayal of the dying Agrippina (mother of the emporer, Nero) by the sculptor, Andrea Vacca.

Agrippina

Antinous / Alexander

At the entrance to the grove, on the right side, in another little niche along the wooded walk, we come to a bust of the youth, Antinous of Claudiopolis, the favorite of the Roman Emporer, Hadrian. After this young man had drowned himself in the Nile, the emperor elevated him to the position of a god, and each year there was a festival in his honor. This bust of Antinous, as well as the one of Alexander the Great on the opposite side, are the works of Verschaffelt.

Apollo

Nearby the Temple of Minerva is another representation of Apollo, this time by the court sculptor, Paul Egell.

Atalantas

Under the trees, which flank both sides of the castle, we find lead sculptures of two Atalantas, works of the Heidelberg sculptor, Heinrich Charaksy. On the north side is the Arcadian Atalanta who had downed a wild boar while on a Calydonian hunt; on the south side the Boeotian Atalanta, who was able to win all of the footraces against her suitors except for the one against Hippomenes. He was able to outwit her with the help of the goddess, Aphrodite, by dropping three golden apples along the path.

Bacchus

At the peripherie of the birdbath is a statue of the young Bacchus which was created by Andrea Vacca.

The Bacchus Children

The Bacchus Children

A few steps farther from Pan, we see a delightful rococo work of art, the Bacchus children playing with a goat. The artist is Konrad Linck, who had already made a name for himself as a modeler in the famous porcelain works at Frankenthal (near Mannheim).

The Earth

The Four Elements

On the lawns behind the stag-pond one sees the statuesque symbols of the four elements: earth, water, fire, and air. Cybele, the mother of the gods and goddess of fertility of the earth, is represented by a lion and a horn of plenty. Neptune, the god of water und the oceans, is seen leaning on a huge fish. Vulcan wears his Phrygian cap on his head and is provided with the attributes of fire. Juno, goddess of the moon, floats on clouds together with the peacock which was dedicated to her. All of these, as well as the lead vases and the urns in the immediate vicinity, were originated by Verschaffelt.

The Springtime

The Four Seasons

Along the path which leads by the canal there are two allegorical figures representing springtime and summer by an unknown artist from Lorraine; the figure which represents winter stands at the opposite end on the other side of the canal. The one representing autumn is no longer extant.

Galatea

This is a particularly beautiful and romantic portion of the gardens. Just a few steps away from Pan we find the wonderful piece of sculpture of Galatea, a marble statue by Gabriel de Grupello. The artist shows this beautiful woman preparing to enter the bath. At her feet we see an old Triton who is wooing her, and is in the act of handing her a wreath of shells and pearls.

Justitia

At the crossing of the paths, which close off the portion of the lawns near the stag group is a statue of Justitia by Gabriel Grupello.

Mercury

Nearby the Temple of Minerva is a statue of Mercury by Grupello.

Galatea

Mercury

The Memorial Stones

Located not far from the statue of Agrippina, we find two memorial stones there, both of which were put into the ground by Carl Theodore. The first is in memory of Romans and Germans, whose bones, urns, weapons, and other utensils were found during the con-

Memorial Stone

struction period in 1765. The other stone bears the following inscription, which is of interest to the visitor: „You admire, wanderer! She herself is astonished, she who denied it, the great mother of things, nature." And on the back of the stone a second inscription: „Carl Theodore created this for himself and his own people for purposes of recreation and respite from the daily tasks. This monument be placed here in 1771." Although this inscription may have originally appeared to have been a bit of conceited praise of himself, it has turned out to be the historical and artistic truth. It is true that many individuals shared in the creation of this bit of paradise, which at first was denied by nature. But in the end it was nature that com-

pleted this vast work. The trees have now grown to full size, and have become a very important part of the park. The gardens would have lost much of their effect, were it not for the stately rows of linden and chestnut trees. The chestnut blossoms enrich the scenery in May, and the sweet scent of the linden trees can be experienced late in June. It took many years of growth, and nature's help, before the English Garten portion came into its own. And throughout most of the year flowers can be seen in bloom. And so it was nature, after all, which put a crowning effect on this artistic accomplishment.

Without a doubt the Elector Carl Theodore is the great inspirator of the park. We are not sure just how much he personally collaborated in the project. We do know that he was a very cultured and artistic person. This view is supported by the fact that he employed the best architects, landscape architects, and artists of his time.

Minerva

Nearby the temple of Minerva in a little niche along one of the paths,

Minerva

is another statue of Minerva, also by Grupello. Behind Galatea, there is a bust of Minerva which has been set on an old column said to date from an old church near Weinheim built during the time of Charlemagne. The sculptor of Minerva is believed to be Charasky.

Obelisk

In the Arboricum Theodoricum there is an obelisk nearly fifty feet in height, which was placed there in 1777 to mark a graveyard of the Alemannian-Franks dug up during the period of construction.

In the linden promenade which consists of ten rows of linden trees running in a line from north to south, we find four large obelisks near the Arion fountain.

The Great Pan

Pan, the Arcadian god of the shepherds, is seen sitting on a small, rocky ledge in a niche in the woods. It is one of the finest works of art in the gardens. The artist was the Mannheim sculptor, Simon Peter Lamine. Pan is seen playing on his pipe, and one has the feeling that one can hear his tempting melody. The god of the shepherds and the forests has a mocking smile on his lips. But this Pan is not only the god of the shepherds. He represents two additional personalities. He is the Greek Satyr, the robber of the nymphs. He is also the Roman Faunus, with head and body of a man and legs of a goat, fond of riotous merriment and lustful of nature. Thus Pan is the smiling seducer of the Schwetzingen park.

Pan

The River-Gods

The Rhine

It is at the lake that the imposing symbol figures of the Rhine and the Danube are to be found. These are also considered to be among the best works of Verschaffelt. The artist had wanted to portray all four rivers which flowed through the territory of the Elector, but he died in 1793, before he was able to complete figures representing the other two rivers, the Moselle and the Maas.

The Danube

Urns

On the first terrace, quite near the entrance to the park, there are four decorative urns with symbolical portrayals of the hunt, agriculture, horticulture, and the art of warfare. They are early works of the Flemish artist, Verschaffelt, who entered the service of the Electors of the Palatinate in 1752, and later became the director of the electoral art academy in Mannheim.

Very close by Pan are two additional representations of love. There are two lead vases with doves billing and cooing.

Near the Temple of Minerva eight beautiful lead vases also can be seen along the path.

Urn and Obelisk in the French Garden

Urns in the French Garden

The Town of Schwetzingen with the eastern part beyond the Railway

Of Counts of the Palatinate and Electors

Ludwig III caried out the sentence of the Council of Constanze against the Bohemian religious reformer, John Huss. Huss was burned at the stake on June 6, 1415, and the tragic consequences were the Hussite wars, which lasted for decades and which laid waste half of Germany. Religious peace was not established until 1485, with the settlement at Kuttenberg.

The older son of Ludwig III was known as Frederick I the Victorious. He was populary called „Palatinate Fritz". Frederick was one of the most capable rulers of the Palatinate. In 1462 he defeated the army of the Elector Adolf of Nassau at Seckenheim; and he was not at all ruffled when he was excommunicated by the pope. Nor did he pay any more attention to the fact that he had been placed under a ban by the emperor. He had married Clara Dettin, the daughter of a wealthy patrician family from Augsburg. In his old age he became a barefooted monk in Heidelberg.

The Protestant Elector Frederick V (who was married to the Stuart Princess Elisabeth, daughter of King James of England), proclaimed himself king of Bohemia. However, he was defeated by an army of the Catholic League in 1620, and was forced to flee from the Palatinate.

Elector Karl Ludwig (1618-1680) was forced to spend his youth in Holland and England, in exile. He was still in England when his uncle, Charles I, died on the gallows. He was not able to return to the Palatinate until 1649, one year after the signing of the Treaty of Westphalia, ending the Thirty Years' War. He was then thirty-two years of age. The ill fortune during his youth helped to make him a very capable ruler. He rebuilt the devastated areas of his realm. His ministers found him to be unrelenting, but his people loved him for his mildness. He performed the almost

Friedrich V.

RICHARD BELLM

Sketchbook of Heidelberg
in German and English

CAROLVS LVDOVICVS COMES PALAT. AD
Rhen. S. Rom. Imp. Archi-Thesaur. Princ.
Elect. Dux Bavar. etc.

Karl Ludwig

miraculous feat of taxing the populace at the unbelievably low rate of one percent, and yet his treasury was always filled. By the time of his death, the state's income was higher than during the period immediately preceding the wars, showing how quickly and how well the countryside had recovered from the blight of war.

And once again, Pan began to play his great... his greatest... and most beautiful song of love in Schwetzingen, which moved the heart of all Europe, just as the devilish game of politics and war had done a few years before.

In 1650, the Elector married Charlotte, the daughter of Amalie, Landgravine of Hessen. This Family had been closely allied with Gustavus Adolfus and the French during the Thirty Years' War. The marriage of these two individualists – she, a thoroughly experienced but headstrong, dicorial, and quarrelsome woman – he, at least as egotistic as his wife, and also nervous and irritable as the result of the taxing job of governing – had an unhappy ending. After the birth of their third child, the two separated, in spite of the attemps of friends and neighboring rulers to bring about a reconciliation at the Diet of Regensburg. In the meantime Karl Ludwig had fallen in love with Luise von Degenfeld, a young lady-in-waiting to Charlotte. There is a piquant touch to this fantastic love story in that the Elector began the relationship by writing love-letters in Latin. Not until later was it discovered that they were not original, but had been copied out of a novel by Aeneas Silvias Piccolomini, who became Pope Pius II (apparently Karl Ludwig had no time to busy himself with original letters in Latin). If we can believe the chronicles of his time, the Elector decided upon a sensational step, as a result of pressure on the part of Luise's brother. Instead of having her as his mistress, he decided upon marriage, although he had not divorced Charlotte. He then elevated Luise to the rank of Raugrave, a title equivalent to that of a countess, but no longer in use. The family, which had received it from the German emperors centuries before, had long since died out.

And so begins in Schwetzingen a romance which puts to shame every modern love story, even those on our stages and in the films. Karl Ludwig had the Schwetzingen castle rebuilt for Luise, and in the spring of 1657 the couple moved into their new home und lived there happily for twenty years. It was the moving drama of two human beings which transcended the moral concepts and conventions of their time. Thirteen children were born during this moranatic marriage. Luise died at the birth of her fourteenth child, on March 18, 1677. The Elector mourned over her death, and erected a church (called Holy Concord) in her memory. It was destroyed a few years later by the French during the Orleanic Wars of Succession. Luise's untimely passing left the Elector broken in spirit, and he soon became an old man.

Even before his death, Karl Ludwig experienced the horrors of war. The Palatinate had scarcely been restored, when Louis XIV demanded help in the second war of conquest against Holland. Soon after the Elector had refused his assistance, the French occupied the Palatinate. Schwetzingen became the headquarters für General de Turennes. Karl Ludwig, whose troops were stationed in Mannheim, challenged the famous French general to a duel on July 11, 1674. Instead of accepting, the Frenchman replied that, since he had the honor of serving the Kings of France, he would fight at the head of 20000 seconds. Schwetzingen was spared from any serious devastation on that occasion. Generel de Turennes was killed a

year later near Sasbach (Black Forest), where his monument may be seen today, built on a piece of exterritioral property belonging to France.

And once again we find that Schwetzingen's fate is linked to the name of a woman.

The daughter of Karl Ludwig and Charlotte, Elisabeth Charlotte, married the Duke of Orleans, brother of Louis XIV in 1671. This was a purely political marriage. Karl Ludwig's aim was to effect a bond of friendship between France und the Palatinate, thereby assuring peace and quiet on his western border. „Liselotte of the Pfalz", as Elisabeth Charlotte was popularly

Elisabeth Charlotte

called, was very much attached to Schwetzingen. In many of her Letters to Luise, whom she was very fond of, she would inquire about the park and her favorite birds, the nightingales. Although her visits were rate, she one wrote: „I shall never forget Heidelberg, Mann-

Rastatt Castle

heim, and Schwetzingen. Schwetzingen is a lovely place which I always loved. I can remember it, as though I were standing in front of it, looking at it with my own eyes."

One of the mist heartbreaking periods of history was about to begin. These were the nine years of slaughter called the Orleanic Wars of Succession which took place in the Palatinate, against the will of Liselotte. We can imagine how she must have felt, when she heard that her brother-in-law's armies had invaded her homeland and were destroying everything in sight.

After Karl Ludwig's death in 1680, his son, Karl II, became the ruler of the Palatinate, but died five years later without an heir. According to the law of succession, the Palatinate was to become a possession of the Palatinate-Neuburg rulers, whose court was at Duesseldorf.

The Elector Karl Philipp (1716–1742), Johann Wilhelm's successor, got into difficulty with the citizens of Heidelberg because of the Church of the Holy Ghost (situated at the marketplace directly across from the famous Hotel Ritter), which had been divided into two parts in order to allow both the Protestants and the Catholics to worship there. The Elector had wanted to return the entire church to the Catholics, but the Reformed groups opposed this. According to the reports dating from these times, the wall which divided the two religious groups in the church „stirred half of Europe's diplomatic corps." The Elector left

Arms of the Counts of the Palatinate

Heidelberg in a rage (1720), transferred his court to Mannheim, and there he built Europe's largest palace which was almost completely destroyed during the last war. As the palace was not completed until 1731, Karl Philipp temporarily resided in the Schwetzingen castle. During this brief period of residence there, he added several touches to the park. For one thing, he transferred the Orangery from Duesseldorf, and it is reported that the park bore a strong resemblance to an orange and lemon plantation. He also built an attractive greenhouse in the middle of the gardens, where the main fountains are now located. The walls of this building were decorated with precious porcelain from Delft. A covered corridor connected the greenhouse with the castle. But all this has since disappeared.

The Elector died without any heirs, and so the rule of the House of Palatinate-Neuburg came to an end. In 1743 the Elector Carl Theodore took over the reins of government.

The residence of Rastatt was built by Margrave Ludwig Wilhelm of Baden-Baden as the »new castle« according to the architecturel ideas in 1700 in Germany. Especially at this place you can find the baroque arrangement of castle and town in its original form.

Carl Theodore

The Last Grandseigneur

Carl Theodore

Who was this man Carl Theodore, the creator of the Schwetzingen gardens, whose name we encounter again and again in descriptions of the park?

Carl Theodore, of the Palatinate-Sulzbach line, a collateral line of the Wittelsbacher, was born 10 December 1724 in Castle Drogenbusch near Brussels. His father died at the early age of 34, and Carl Theodore became Prince Elector of the Palatinate at the age of 10, since his hereditary uncle, the Elector Karl Philipp, had no children. During his lifetime, the old Elector delegated some of the business of government to his nephew by turning over to him administration of the Duchy of Sulzbach and some other territory of minor importance. In order to complete the transfer of title, the youth had to be declared officially of age, which was done by the Emperor on 10 July 1741. The Elector took a great deal of interest in the education of his heir and considered it important that he devote himself to a study of the military aspects of his land. „At the same time he had neither the qualifications nor the inclination for the military, the less so as he had come to realize from his studies of history and from the political events of his time that only the larger powers could be military nations; the smaller states had far more to gain from political acuteness than from weapons", says the historian Lipowski. At the age of 18, Carl Theodore was married to Elisabeth Auguste, a granddaughter of Karl Philipp, who was four years older than he. Six months later Karl Philipp, of whom his subjects always said they mourned his life but not his death, died at the age of 80 years, and on New Year's Day, 1743, Carl Theodore assumed control of the government at the youthful age of 18.

It cannot be said that Carl Theodore's inheritance was particularly prepossessing. The court, to be sure, created an impression of wealth and splendor, but the land itself was poor, and its economic life almost non-existent. The young

Maulbronn Monastery

Carl Theodore did his best to help his land and his subjects. The Heidelberg historian, Friedrich Christoph Schlosser, who was the first to describe the era of absolutism in his famous history of the eighteenth century, has little good to say of Carl Theodore's reign. He does admit, however, that "in the beginning Carl Theodore showed an inclination to thrift which the Palatinate had not seen in a long time". In the final analysis, Schlosser has given us a condemnation of the period and its rule and – writing in the heyday of Kant's doctrine of ethics – it is perhaps natural that he should reproach Carl Theodore with every single fault. Haeusser, his disciple, does nothing to change this highly moralizing portraits of Carl Theodore, and the resulting impression of him as a Biedermeier prince who let himself be guided by Jesuits, by his

father confessor, by a host of mistresses, and – lastly – by his own ruthless and egocentric intelligence, which had no thought but of his own personal advantage, is not one which rouses our sympathies. More objective critics, such as Stephan von Stengel, point to the prince's genial nature, to his love of order in everything he did, and to his punctuality and reliability. He was a ruler who really worked! Carl Theodore von Heigel, who criticizes the Elector severely, admits that "there can be no doubt that the fame of his name and the splendor of his court were not the chief motives of the Elector's work; he was deeply sincere in his desire to increase the welfare of his people by the introduction of sensible measures". The fact that his choise of political advisors and helpers was not always fortunate, that he was cheated and deceived, that political jobbery ran rife (although it was expressly forbidden by the Elector), and that appointments as professors, judges, and high court officials could be had for money – all this is another story. However, we cannot judge those times of 200 years ago by the same criteria in use today. They had their own political, economic, and social usages and norms.

In the older literature, a great deal of interest is devoted to the amorous exploits of the Elector. After all, he was the central figure of his own little world, and this world did not hesitate to make public his affairs with the Mannheim baker-master Huber's daugh-

Elisabeth Auguste

In Maulbronn you find one the best preserved and most impressive monasteries of medieval times, north of the Alpes. It is a document of the monastic spirit of the Cisterian order which has stayed and worked at this place for 390 years until 1537.

ter (whom he made Countess Bergstein), with the dancer Josepha Seyffert (whom he elevated to the nobility with title of Countess Heydeck, and whose children became countesses and princes of the realm at Bretzenheim), with Baroness Elisabeth Schenk von Castel, with Countess Josephine von Toerring-Seefeld, with the lovely Auguste Wendling (whose praises were sung by the poets Wieland, Heinse, and Iffland), and with the Baronesse von Leutrum. Carl Theodore's lovelife, like of all the rulers of his days, was richly varied.

Carl Theodore's faithlessness was a source of great unhappiness to his wife, Elisabeth Auguste. On 28 June 1761, she gave birth to an heir, Franz Josef Ludwig, at Schwetzingen; however, the child died shortly after birth. The marriage which was not a particularly happy one, produced no further offspring. In 1768 Elisabeth Auguste moved to Oggersheim, in the Palatinate, where she founded a pilgrimage church and devoted herself to good works as a pious and well-loved mother of her country. She died in 1794 at Weinheim.

The political situation which the young Carl Theodore inherited with his throne was an extremely difficult one, and it required all of his political acumen to preserve the Palatinate. Its military forces were weak, and the geographical spread of its territory, extending from Duesseldorf and Juelich to Neuburg on the Danube and to Weiden in the forests of Bohemia,

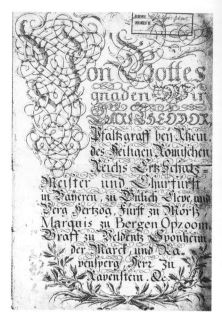

Titles of Carl Theodore

left it unprotected in the midst of the spheres of influence of France, Austria and Prussia. The reign of Carl Theodore saw the three Silesian Wars between Frederick II and Austria, the Bavarian War of Succession (1778), and the first Coalition War against revolutionary France, during the last of which the Palatinate was once again the scene of fighting. Although the Elector was unable to keep the horror of war completely outside the borders of his land, it must be admitted, to his great credit, that the fifty-seven years of his rule were years of peace. Frederick the Great of Prussia often termed his colleague on the Mannheim throne a "lucky dog" in this respekt. After Carl Theodore had inherited Bavaria, upon the death of Maxi-

Favorite Castle

milian Josef in 1777, Old Fritz made the following comment: "Without drawing his sword even once that lazy fellow has gained more territory than I have been able to in three wars, one of which lasted seven years"!

Frederick was one of Carl Theodore's political opponents. In 1778 he started the Bavarian War of Succession because Carl Theodore had indicated his willingness to turn over his Bavarian inheritance to the Habsburgs. This rather unusual war (the so-called „Potato War"), in which the Prussians lost 8000 men through sickness and desertion and in which no real fighting took place, was concluded on 13 May 1779 by the Peace of Teschen, whereby Austria was awarded the territory along the Inn.

Carl Theodore, who moved his residence to Munich in 1778, was never particularly happy with his Bavarian inheritance. He was not popular among the Bavarians and he never really felt at home there. In 1785, Emperor Josef II of Austria again brought up the plan of turning Bavaria over to the House of Habsburg, and in exchange offered Carl Theodore the so-called Austrian Netherlands, the territory which is today Belgium. Both Russia and France were persuaded to concur in this plan; Frederick II frustrated it by founding the Federation of German Princes.

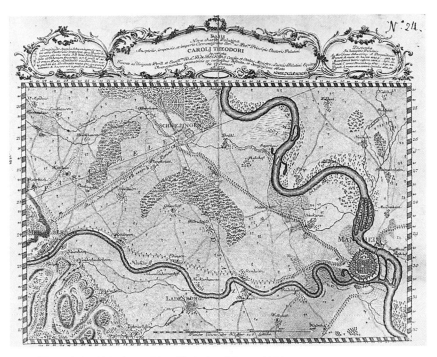

"New Map of the Palatinate" by Christian Mayer 1776

(near Baden-Baden) is a jewel among the baroque castle buildings at the Upper Rhine-River. It was built in the 18th century for Margravine Sibylla Augusta as a summer residence. Remarkable is the interior (pottery, bone china and fayence art).

DAS SCHWEZINGER SCHLOSS. | LE CHATEAU DE SCHWEZINGEN.

Bei F. Schwab in Schwezingen.

Lithography of the Castle

Carl Theodore's plan, the founding of a large state bounded by the Rhine, Meuse, and Shelde Rivers, opens up a tremendous political perspective – a nation unified both economically and geographically, ruled by a common political system and served by a centralized system of communications and traffic, and peopled by a highly-civilized folk in which the intelligent Rhine-Frankish element would hold a position of natural superiority over the fringe minorities (Flemish and Walloon peoples with whom they were bound by close racial ties).

In 1781 Emperor Josef II of Austria made a visit to Schwetzingen under the incognito of Count von Falkenstein and was taken on a tour of the park by the court architect, Pigage. On this occasion the Emperor made several remarks of a political nature, which are of great interest in the light of subsequent developments. Their conversation is preserved for us in an original manuscript by Pigage:

The Emperor commented to his companion as follows: „Truly, Sir, I am excited to ever greater admiration! It is quite incomprehensible to me that the Elector can choose to give up such a delightful residence as the Palatinate – it is in itself a garden, an earthly paradise."

Pigage: „Count, the reason for it is that Bavaria is his biggest piece of cake at the moment, and it is natural that he prefers it."

Bruchsal Castle

The Emperor: „True, one eats both big and little cakes wherever one likes. But as far as I am concerned, if I were your Elector, I would eat all of my cakes in the Palatinate."

Carl Theodore had relatively little chance to eat his cake in the Palatinate after this, for his visits to Mannheim and Schwetzingen, always an occasion of rejoicing for the populace, were few and far between. On 15 February 1795 (six months after Elisabeth Auguste's death), the seventy year-old Elector married the Archduchess Maria Leopoldine of Austria-Este-Modena, a girl of eighteen. On 12 February 1799 he suffered a stroke while playing cards, and he died on 16 February. A niche in the Theatiner Church in Munich contains the coffin with the last earthly remains of this „Louis XIV." of the Palatinate. What has remained from the period of Carl Theodore? What remains of his work?

Northern Circle-House

That which is timeless: the cultural heritage of the German nation!

By this we do not mean the fairyland gardens of Schwetzingen alone; Carl Theodore also completed the castle at Mannheim, the largest castle in Europe. It was destroyed by bombardment during the war, and is now being rebuilt. He collected a library of more than 100,000 volumes, founded a collection of antiquities, established an academy of sciences, and the physical economy society; he built the observatories in Schwetzingen and Mannheim, founded an academy of fine arts and the association of surgeons; he established the so-called „Deutsche Gesellschaft" (German Society), whose purpose was to spread the use of good taste, to standardize the German language and at the same time to study its various dialects. In Mannheim he built a department stored, the Jesuit Church, the Armory and the National Theater, which was Schiller's theater and a cultural shrine for the entire world. Mannheim in Carl Theodore's time was the avante-garde leader in the fields of German drama and music; it was here that Stamitz and Richter founded the „Mannheim School", with its new orchestral techniques, which was to be the fore-runner of the new style, Classicism. In Munich, Carl Theodore began the art collection from which was to grow the Pinakothek. And this list of Carl Theodore's cultural heritage is far from exhausted.

The residence of Prince-Bishop Damian Hugo of Schönborn was built in the 18th century. The extraordinary centra staircase was planned by Balthasar Neumann.

Carl Theodore was a man of universal culture, the last grand seigneur in Germany, a sovereign prince and ruler of the Palatinate, a patron of the arts, a darling of the Muses, and a friend of the sciences; he might well have descended from the Mount Parnassus of ancient tradition.

And not even the parasites and ne'er-do-wells of his court, for whom he had done so much, came to weep at his grave.

We have reason to be grateful to him. Nearly two hundred years after his death, this fortunate land on the Upper Rhine still bears the signs of the rich and thriving culture which is so apparent in the park of Schwetzingen.

We have all lost a great deal in the fiery holocausts of war; still, we have this enchanted and enchant-

Interior of the Castle

ing garden as a precious heritage and a national possession of great value.

It was not turned into a museum, but has remained a joyous part of our everyday life.

The Castle

Dilsberg Stronghold

The Artists

When we speak of the Schwetzingen gardens we must not forget the many artists who participated in its creation and completion. The great designer from Lorraine, Nicolas de Pigage, and his three chief assistants, the landscape architects, Johann Ludwig Petri, van Wynder, and Johann Wilhelm Sckell.

Allessandro Galli da Bibiena

And then the elite group of sculptors: the Heidelberger, Heinrich Charasky; Barthélemy Guibal, of Lorraine; the Italians, de Grupello, Andrea Vacca, and Francesco Carabelli; the Germans, van den Branden, Paul Egell, Simon Lamine, Konrad Linck, Franz Xaver Messerschmidt; the Flemish master, Peter Anton von Verschaffelt; the Italien stucco artists, Pozzi and Albucci; the painters, Guibal and Kobell, and many others. It is, of course, no wonder that the Schwetzingen park has been a great attraction down through the generations. Furthermore, a sizable number of volumes has been written about it. Just to count up the names of the famous, who visited here, would take many pages. Voltaire and Gluck were here; Mozart played in the gardens as a child (1763), and Schiller was inspired to write his „Don Carlos". In today's world, where practically nobody has time for anything, it is a quiet island on which one can find peace, and rest, and relaxation, and perhaps even inspiration.

Peter Anton von Verschaffelt

Nicolas de Pigage

Dilsberg Stronghold, situated at the Neckar River, is an interesting background for concerts and theatre performances.

The Town of Schwetzingen with its Hotels and Shops

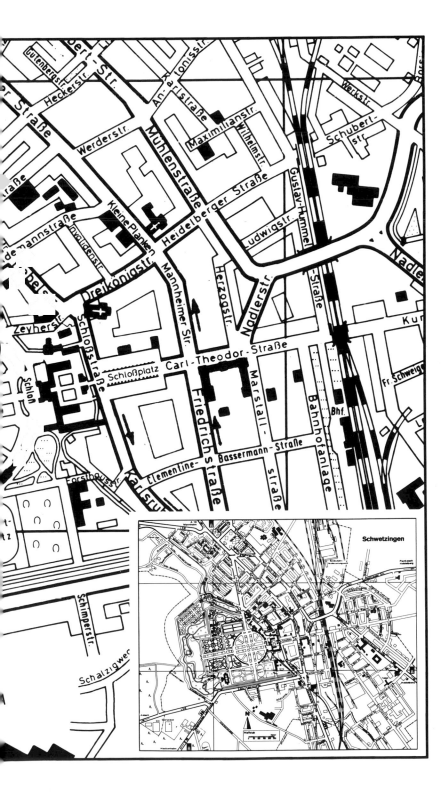

Restaurants · Cafés

Achat Hotel am Schloßgarten
Schälzigweg 1-3, Tel. 206-0, Fax 206-333

Alexander Grill
Lindenstraße 46, Telefon 3650

Bellamar-Restaurant
Odenwaldring, Telefon 16779, Fax 29278

Blaues Loch
Zeyherstraße 3, Telefon 21360

Café Journal
Karlsruher Str. 1, Tel. 9327-0, Fax 932793

Chinesische Mauer
Markgrafenstraße 2-8, Telefon 26688

Eintracht
Heidelberger Straße 14, Telefon 3315

El Greco
Mannheimer Straße 35, Telefon 4580

Falkenhof
Bahnhofanlage 14, Tel. 12024, Fax 270010

Fäß'l
Mannheimer Str. 41, Telefon 13080

Frankeneck
Friedr.-Ebert-Str. 36, Tel. 3323, Fax 270271

Goldener Drache
Lindenstraße 20, Telefon 24420

Grüner Baum
Carl-Theodor-Str. 2, Tel. 4362, Fax 270966

Greenhouse Bistro Café
Clementine-Bassermann-Str. 15, Tel. 17588

Helga's Steakhouse
Herzogstraße 31, Tel. 15961, Fax 270856

Adler-Post Hotel Restaurant
Schloßstraße 3, Tel. 10036-37, Fax 21442

Kaffeehaus
Schloßplatz 3, Telefon 12170, Fax 24584

Kühler Krug
Wildemannstraße 5, Telefon 4818

Laugeweck
Herzogstraße 29, Telefon 4121

Kurfürstenstube Café-Bistro
Schloßeingang, Telefon 14656, Fax 10726

Löwe Romantik Hotel
Schloßstraße 4-6, Tel. 2809-0, Fax 10726

Lügebrückl
Hebelstraße 15, Telefon 10028

Maharaja Tandoori Restaurant
Friedrichsstr. 1, Tel. 923067, Fax 14527

Mamma Rosa Ristorante
Dreikönigstraße 6, Telefon 4535

Pazza's Garden
Zähringerstr. 5, Tel. 21521, Fax 13882

Pizzeria Pazza
Marstallstraße 18, Tel. 4943, Fax 13882

Pomp Restaurant Bistro
Dreikönigstraße 6, Telefon 4307

Ritter
Schloßplatz 1, Tel. 93300, Fax 933030

Schloßrestaurant im Schloß Schwetzingen
Telefon 12020

Shakespeare
Kronenstraße 2, Telefon und Fax 13558

Shanghai China-Restaurant
Carl-Theodor-Straße 7, Telefon 17533

Am Stadion
Ketscher Landstr. 11, Tel. 271638, Fax 930277

Tennisclub Blau-Weiß
Odenwaldring 2, Telefon 12551

Welde-Stammhaus
Mannheimer Str. 2a, Tel. und Fax 4830

Werner's Bar-Bistro
Schloßstraße 6, Telefon 2809-0, Fax 10726

Zagreb Hotel Restaurant
Robert-Bosch-Str. 9, Tel. 2840, Fax 284200

Hotels · Guesthouses

Hotel Adler-Post
Schloßstraße 3, Tel. 1 00 36-37, Fax 2 14 42

Hotel Berlin
Liselottestraße 22, Telefon 2 50 34-35

Hotel zum Erbprinzen
Karlsruher Str. 1, Tel. 93 27-0, Fax 93 27 93

Hotel-Restaurant Falkenhof
Bahnhofanlage 14, Tel. 1 20 24, Fax 27 00 10

Achat Hotel am Schloßgarten
Schälzigweg 1-3, Tel. 2 06-0, Fax 2 06-3 33

Romantik Hotel Löwe
Schloßstraße 4-6, Tel. 28 09-0, Fax 1 07 26

Hotel Ramada
Carl-Benz-Str. 1, Tel. 2 81-0, Fax 2 81-2 22

Hotel Shakespeare Bistro + Café
Kronenstr. 2, Tel. 27 09 94, Fax 1 35 58

Hotel am Stadion
Ketscher Landstr. 11, Tel. 93 0 20, Fax 93 02 77

Hotel am Theater
Hebelstraße 15, Telefon 1 00 28, Fax 1 36 99

Villa Guggolz Hotel Garni
Zähringer Str. 51, Tel. 2 50 47, Fax 2 50 49

Hotel Zagreb
Robert-Bosch-Str. 9, Tel. 28 40, Fax 28 42 00

Badner Hof
Bismarckstr. 1, Telefon 34 71

Gasthof zum Ritter
Schloßplatz 1, Tel. 9 33 00, Fax 93 30 30

Gasthof Mainzer Rad
Marktplatz 4, Tel. 45 24, Fax 1 40 07

Gaststätte Zum Rheintal
Marktplatz 30, Telefon 1 57 30

Helga's Steakhouse
Herzogstraße 31, Tel. 1 59 61, Fax 27 08 56

Kaiser-Friedrich
Luisenstraße 18, Telefon 1 33 65

Pension Brenner
Kl. Krautgärten 5, Tel. 93 1 70 + 2 55 23, Fax 93 17 19

Pension Seitz
Zeyherstraße 3, Telefon 2 60 77

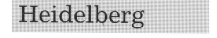
Heidelberg

The Castle △

The Heidelberg Castle was the first residence of the Electors of the Palatinate. The building of the castle took more than four centuries to complete. In 1764 the castle was struck by lightning and seriously damaged. The romantic ruin serves as background for the castle-festival during the summer months. Places of interest are as well the Great Vat in the castle's cellar and the Pharmaceutical Museum in the Ottheinrich Building.

Mannheim

The Castle ▽

The castle was built by the Electors of the Palatinate Carl Philipp and Carl Theodor at the beginning of the 18th century. The residence in the style of French castles was damaged in the Second World War. The rebuilt castle houses today faculties of the Mannheim University. The Hall of Knights is used for celebrations, honor ceremonies and concerts.

Speyer Cathedral

Bruchsal Castle

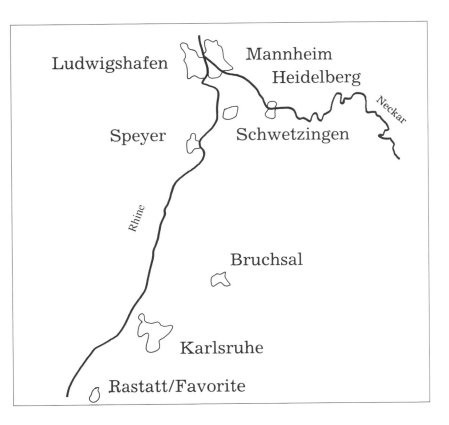

Ludwigshafen

Mannheim

Heidelberg

Neckar

Speyer

Schwetzingen

Rhine

Bruchsal

Karlsruhe

Rastatt/Favorite

Karlsruhe Castle

Rastatt Castle

SCHWETZINGEN FESTIVAL

Opera · concert · drama
ballet · chamber music · oratorio

Week of encounter for young artists

Every year in May and June

Information:
Ticket Service Schwetzinger Zeitung
Phone 06202/205-0